RECYCLING
35mm
CANISTERS
for the
TEACHING
of
SCIENCE

ALFRED De VITO

PROFESSOR EMERITUS OF SCIENCE EDUCATION

PURDUE UNIVERSITY

CREATIVE VENTURES, INC.
P. O. Box 2286
West Lafayette, Indiana 47906

Library of Congress Cataloging in Publication Data

De Vito, Alfred

   RECYCLING 35mm CANISTERS FOR THE TEACHING OF SCIENCE

Current Printing (last digit)

10 9 8 7 6 5 4 3 2

ISBN: 0-942034-08-2

Printed in the United States of America

FOREWORD

THIS IS A BOOK ABOUT THE CREATIVE USE OF 35mm CANISTERS
FOR USE IN SCIENCE INSTRUCTION. MATERIALS FOR SCIENCE INSTRUC-
TION AT THE ELEMENTARY AND MIDDLE SCHOOL LEVELS ARE OFTEN EX-
PENSIVE AND SCARCE. THEY ARE ALSO DIFFICULT TO STORE, CLEAN,
AND MAINTAIN. WNENEVER AVAILABLE FREE OR INEXPENSIVE, DISPOS-
ABLE MATERIALS SHOULD BE USED. THESE ATTRIBUTES ALLOW FOR MORE
MATERIALS TO BE PLACED IN THE HANDS OF CHILDREN. THUS EACH CHILD
CAN BECOME MORE DIRECTLY INVOLVED IN HANDS-ON ACTIVITIES AND EX-
PERIMENTS THAT MAY FOLLOW.

ACCEPTING THE NOTION THAT ALL OF US ARE BETTER THAN ANY ONE
OF US, THE NUMEROUS IDEAS AND ACTIVITIES THAT ARE PRESENTED HERE
SERVE MERELY AS SPRINGBOARDS TO THE MANY IDEAS THAT YOU AND YOUR
STUDENTS WILL GENERATE.

THE AUTHOR HAS SOME NOTES, COMMENTS, AND CAUTIONS, THESE ARE:
REMEMBER NOTHING IN SCIENCE WORKS. NOTHING WORKS WELL.
NOTHING WORKS LIKE AUTHORS SAY THEY DO. THAT IS, UNLESS
YOU, LIKE AUTHORS, MAKE THEM WORK. AND, THEREIN LIES THE
CHALLENGE. NEVER FAIL, ONE-HUNDRED PERCENT, ACCURATE, EVERY-
TIME ACTIVITIES ARE ALMOST NON-EXISTENT. IF THEY DO OCCUR,
THEY ARE USUALLY DULL, AND THEY DEPRIVE THE INVESTIGATOR OF
THE CREATIVE PLEASURES ASSOCIATED WITH SEARCHING OUT ONE'S
OWN SOLUTIONS. THUS, THE INVESTIGATOR IS DEPRIVED OF THAT
WHICH IS MOST GERMANE TO SCIENCE. THE EXPLORATION OF ALL
THE VARIABLES IN ANY GIVEN ACTIVITY USUALLY FAR EXCEEDS THE
SPACE AND TIME CONSTRAINTS PROVIDED BY AUTHORS. AUTHORS

PLANT SEEDS, THEY DON'T NECESSARILY CULTIVATE THE GARDEN.
TEACHERS EXERCISE THE SAME PREROGATIVE. ACTIVITIES ARE
DOORWAYS TO THE RESOLUTION OF PROBLEMS OR QUESTIONS
THROUGH EXPERIMENTATION.

NOT ALL 35mm CANISTERS ARE ALIKE. MOST ARE MADE OF
PLASTIC. SOME ARE MADE OF METAL. SOME ARE OPAQUE. SOME
ARE TRANSLUCENT. AND, SOME ARE TRANSPARENT. WHILE THEY
ARE ALL CYLINDRICAL, THEIR COVERS VARY. FOR A SPECIFIC
USAGE, EACH CANISTER DISTINCTION HAS ITS OWN ADVANTAGE OR
DISADVANTAGE.   A VALUABLE COMPONENT OF "MAKING IT WORK"
USING WHAT YOU HAVE TO ACCOMPLISH A DESIRED OBJECTIVE IS
PART AND PARCEL TO THE ACT OF SCIENCING. THIS ACT OF IN-
VOLVING ONESELF IN THE SEEKING, SEARCHING, SEIZING ON
IDEAS TO SOLVE A PROBLEM IS A VITAL COMPONENT OF SCIENCING.

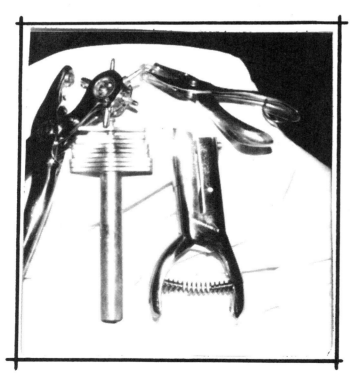

MANY OF THESE AC-
TIVITIES REQUIRE PUNCHING,
CUTTING, OR BORING HOLES
IN PLASTIC. THIS REQUIRES
SOME SIMPLE TOOLS SUCH AS
PAPER PUNCHES, METAL OR
LEATHER PUNCHES, AWLS, DIF-
FERENT SIZE NAILS, AND EVEN
A SET OF CORK BORERS. EACH
TOOL HAS A UNIQUE PURPOSE
AND YOU WILL FIND A USE FOR
EACH. TOOLS ARE DANGEROUS
IF USED INAPPROPRIATELY.
GREAT CARE SHOULD BE TAKEN WHEN USING SHARP TOOLS THAT REQUIRE

THE APPLICATION OF PRESSURE TO CUT OR PUNCH THROUGH VARIOUS
MATERIALS. PLASTIC MATERIALS TEND TO BE SLIPPERY AND CARE
MUST BE EXERCISED WHEN PIERCING THEM. NO ONE NEEDS A 35mm
INJURY!! CHILDREN SHOULD NOT WORK WITH SHARP TOOLS. WHEN
WORKING WITH 35mm CANISTERS WORK SLOWLY, DON'T RUSH, AND
CONCENTRATE ON THE TASK AT HAND. DO NOT USE HEATED OBJECTS
LIKE A NAIL TO BURN A HOLE THROUGH PLASTIC MATERIAL. NOX-
IOUS FUMES MAY BE GIVEN OFF. IF IN DOUBT ABOUT A PROCEDURE,
OBTAIN HELP FROM SOMEONE MORE KNOWLEDGEABLE THAN YOU ABOUT
THE MATERIALS AND THE TOOLS INVOLVED.

CONTENTS

METRIC MEASURES

IN mm, WHAT IS THE WIDTH OF THE FILM?

IN mm, WHAT IS THE VOLUME OF THE 35mm CANISTER? ITS HEIGHT? ITS DIAMETER? ITS CIRCUMFERENCE? ITS MASS WHEN FILLED WITH WATER?

WEIGHTS

KNOWING THE MASS OF AN EMPTY 35mm CANISTER, GLUE PLUS SAND (OR SMALL BBs) CAN BE ADDED TO MAKE KNOWN FIXED UNITS OF MASS SUCH AS 25g, 50g, or 100g WEIGHTS.

METRIC WHEEL - A ROLLING RULER

CALCULATE THE CIRCUMFERENCE OF A 35mm CANISTER. ESTABLISH, BY USING A DOT OF WHITE CORRECTION FLUID OR NAIL POLISH, A POINT OF REFERENCE SO THAT COMPLETE REVOLUTIONS CAN BE OBSERVED AND CALCULATED. ROLL THE CYLINDER THROUGH AN UNKNOWN LINEAR DISTANCE AND COUNT THE ROTATIONS. MULTIPLY THIS TIMES THE CIRCUMFERENCE AND OBTAIN A MEASURE OF THE LINEAR DISTANCE. FRACTIONS OF THE CIRCUMFERENCE, FOR EXAMPLE, ONE QUARTER, ONE HALF, ETC. CAN BE DULY MARKED ON THE CANISTER.

AIR PRESSURE (BERNOULLI)

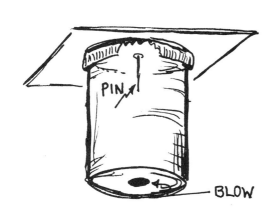

PUNCH OR CUT A 1/4" (APPROXIMATELY) HOLE IN THE CENTER OF THE TOP AND BOTTOM OF THE 35mm CANISTER. FROM A FILING CARD, CUT A THREE INCH SQUARE. FIND THE MID-POINT OF THE SQUARE BY DRAWING DIAGONALS FROM OPPOSING CORNERS. PUSH A PIN THROUGH AT THE INTERSECTION OF THESE TWO LINES. PLACE THE PIN IN THE HOLE OF THE TOP OF THE CLOSED CONTAINER. LIFT THE CONTAINER ABOVE YOUR MOUTH. ATTEMPT TO BLOW THE CARD OUT OF THE CANISTER. TRY THIS AGAIN INVERTING THE CONTAINER WITH THE CARD HELD GENTLY IN PLACE UNTIL YOU START BLOWING THROUGH THE CANISTER. IN BOTH CASES THE CARD WILL REMAIN IN PLACE. THE CARD WILL CLING TO THE CANISTER EVEN AFTER YOU REMOVE YOUR HAND. THE AIR BEING BLOWN OUT FLOWS RAPIDLY BETWEEN THE TOP (OR BOTTOM) OF THE CONTAINER AND THE CARD. THIS PRODUCES A LOW PRESSURE AREA IN THIS SPACE AND THE GREATER PRESSURE AREA ABOVE (OR, IN THE INVERTED AREA, BELOW) THE CARD RETAINS IT IN POSITION.

CONSTELLATION VIEWER

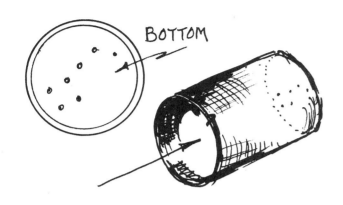

BOTTOM

SELECT A CONSTELLATION. USING WHITE CORRECTION FLUID, PLACE SMALL DOTS, ONE FOR EACH STAR IN YOUR CONSTELLATION, ON THE EXTERIOR BOTTOM OF THE FILM CAN. USING A NAIL OR PICK, CAREFULLY PUSH THROUGH THE PLASTIC BOTTOM AT EACH DOT. VIEWING FROM THE OPEN END, POINTED TOWARDS A LIGHT SOURCE, YOUR CONSTELLATION CAN BE SEEN. MAKE A COLLECTION OF CONSTELLATION VIEWERS. ONE FOR EACH CONSTELLATION.

PLACE A SMALL FLASHLIGHT INSIDE THE CANISTER AND PROJECT THE IMAGE ONTO A SCREEN.

DENSITY · LIQUIDS / SOLIDS

FILL A TRANSPARENT 35mm CANISTER THREE-FOURTHS FILLED WITH OLIVE OIL OR COOKING OIL. PLACE A SMALL CHUNK OF ICE IN THE OIL.

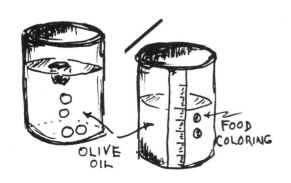

OLIVE OIL

FOOD COLORING

IT WILL FLOAT. THE ICE WILL MELT FORMING INTERESTING WATER GLOBULES AT ITS BASE. THESE EVENTUALLY SINK IN GLOBULAR FASHION TO THE BOTTOM. TRY THIS USING ICE CUBES COLORED WITH FOOD COLORING. THIS MAKES THE OBSERVATION MORE GRAPHIC. REPEAT THIS USING OLIVE OIL AND DROPLETS OF FOOD COLORING ONLY. TAPE A SMALL GRADUATE SCALE TO THE VERTICAL WALL OF THE CYLINDER. ADD FOOD COLORING, ONE DROP AT A TIME. RECORD THE DESCENT. WHAT VARIABLES SUGGEST ADDITIONAL INVESTIGATIONS?

MAGNIFIER / DIRECTION REVERSER

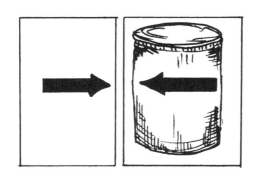

FILL A CLEAR 35mm CANISTER WITH WATER. HOLD THIS IN FRONT OF THE CARD WITH THE ARROW POINTING TO THE RIGHT. ADJUST THE DISTANCE FROM THE CARD SO THAT THE ARROW IS SEEN THROUGH THE FILM CAN POINTING TO THE LEFT. RELATE THIS TO ACTION OF A CAMERA AND THE HUMAN EYE. WHAT DEGREE OF MAGNIFICATION IS OBTAINED AT WHAT DISTANCE? DO ALL LIQUIDS GIVE THE SAME RESULTS? COMPARE THE MAGNIFICATION AND ARROW DIRECTION REVERSAL WHEN THE CONTAINER IS HELD VERTICALLY TO THE ARROW (OR A PRINTED PAGE) OR HELD HORIZONTALLY TO THE ARROW.

STATIC ELECTRICITY

PIERCE THE 35mm CANISTER TOP TO ACCOMODATE PASSAGE OF A PAPER CLIP WIRE. SHAPE A PAPER CLIP INTO A WIRE CONSTRUCT. INSERT THIS THROUGH THE TOP. BEND THE WIRE TO FORM AN "L" AT ITS BASE. HANG A FOLDED PIECE OF ALUMINUM FOIL ON THE "L". CLOSE THE TOP. USE CHARGED OBJECTS (BALLOON, COMB, ETC. RUBBED ON NYLON, WOOL, FUR OR CLOTH)... HOLD THIS AGAINST

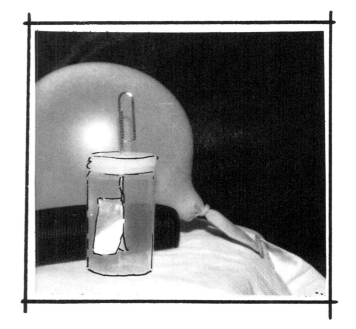

THE TOP OF THE PAPER CLIP. WILL THE INTERIOR ALUMINUM FOIL BE EFFECTED BY TOUCHING THE EXTERIOR OF THE CONTAINER WITH THE CHARGED OBJECTS?

35mm PARACHUTING

CUT SQUARE SECTIONS (START WITH A 16" x 16" SECTION CUT) FROM LARGE GARDEN TYPE GARBAGE BAGS. WITH STRING TIE EACH CORNER TO ONE OF THE HOLES PUNCHED IN THE UPPER PORTION OF A 35mm CANISTER. MAKE THESE HOLES TWO SETS OF OPPOSING HOLES. THROW THIS UP IN THE AIR. DESCRIBE YOUR OBSERVATIONS. WHAT VARIABLES COULD BE CONSIDERED FOR MANIPULATION?

SIMPLE AIR THERMOMETER

PLACE THE PLASTIC TUBE IN A TUMBLER OF COLORED WATER. TEMPERATURE INCREASES EXPAND THE AIR INSIDE THE AIR-FILLED CONTAINER AND FORCES THE LIQUID DOWN IN THE TUBE. FALLING TEMPERATURES CAUSE A REVERSE ACTION.

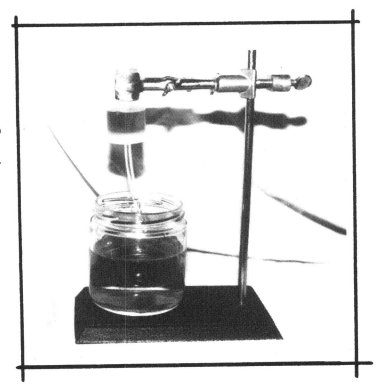

AIR PUCK

NEEDED: A TOPLESS 35mm CANISTER, A BALLOON WITH AN OPENING LARGE ENOUGH TO FIT SNUGLY OVER THE CANISTER OPENING, AN INFLATING NEEDLE USED TO INFLATE ITEMS SUCH AS BASKETBALLS, ETC., AND AN AIR PUMP TO INFLATE THE BALLOON. PIERCE THE BOTTOM OF THE CANISTER FORMING AN OPENING A BIT SMALLER THAN THE DIAMETER OF THE BALL NEEDLE. IN-SERT THE NEEDLE. ATTACH THE AIR PUMP. INFLATE THE BALLOON. AND WHEN IN-FLATED, PULL OUT THE NEEDLE APPARATUS AND HOLD THE CANISTER VERTICALLY AGAINST A TABLE TOP UNTIL THE ESCAPING AIR IN THE BALLOON ALLOWS THE CANISTER AND THE BALLOON TO REMAIN UPRIGHT AND FLOAT ON THE STREAM OF AIR EXHAUSTING FROM THE BALLOON. THIS CUSHION OF AIR

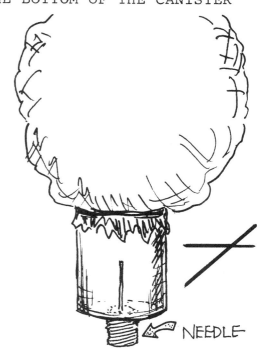

NEEDLE

CAUSES THE APPARATUS TO MOVE IN AN INTERESTING FASHION. IN SOME CASES, YOU MAY WISH TO WEIGHT DOWN THE INTERIOR OF THE CYLINDER TO ASSIST IT TO REMAIN VERTICAL WHILE RIDING ON THE CUSHION OF AIR.

EXPANSION - LIQUID TO A SOLID

FILL A TRANSPARENT 35mm CANISTER (MINUS THE CAP) WITH WATER. DETERMINE THE TOTAL MASS. PLACE THIS IN A FREEZER OVERNIGHT. OBSERVE AND MEASURE CHANGES (IF ANY) IN HEIGHT, MASS, PLUS OTHER PROPERTIES.

PENDULUMS

YOU WILL NEED A 35mm CANISTER, STRING, WEIGHTS OF PREVIOUSLY DETERMINED MASS (BBs, PLUMBER'S CHAIN, FISHING WEIGHTS, WASHERS, ETC.), A RULER, A PROTRACTOR, AND A TIMER. PIERCE THE CAP. THREAD STRING THROUGH THE HOLE AND THEN KNOT THE STRING. INSERT ONE KNOWN WEIGHT INSIDE THE CANISTER. SUSPEND THE CANISTER SO THAT IT CAN SWING FREELY. MEASURE THE LENGTH OF STRING (TRY TO ARRANGE THIS SO THAT THE LENGTH OF STRING COMES OUT TO BE A WHOLE NUMBER).

FROM THE PENDANT POSITION, MOVE THE WEIGHTED CANISTER OUT 20 DEGREES. RELEASE IT. OBSERVE THE MOTION IN TERMS OF DURATION OF SWING, DIRECTION OF SWING, DESCENDING HEIGHT OF THE CANISTER SWING, AND ANY OTHER OBSERVABLE FREQUENCIES. REPEAT THIS, COMPARING INCREASING ANGLES OF RELEASE (MANIPULATED VARIABLE), FOR EXAMPLE, 40 DEGREES, THEN 60 DEGREES, ETC. GRAPH YOUR RESULTS. DOES MANIPULATING THE ANGLE OF RELEASE MAKE A DIFFERENCE? CONSIDER, WITH ALL OTHER VARIABLES HELD CONSTANT, OTHER MANIPULATED VARIABLES, FOR EXAMPLE, LENGTH OF THE STRING, MASS CHANGES, ETC. FROM INFERENCES, GENERATE YOUR VARIOUS HYPOTHESES. ACT, COLLECT DATA, INTERPRET DATA, AND SUPPORT OR REFUTE YOUR PREVIOUSLY STATED HYPOTHESIS.

EARTH SATELLITE

YOU WILL NEED: THREE OPAQUE, 35mm CANISTERS, SOFT CLAY OR WEIGHTS, AND A 120cm LENGTH OF STRING. PIERCE ONE CANISTER TOP.

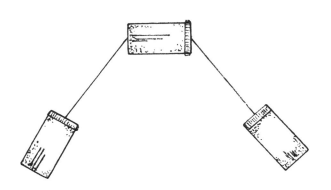

THREAD ONE END OF THE STRING THROUGH THE TOP. KNOT IT SECURELY SO THAT IT WILL NOT PULL OUT WHEN PRESSURE IS APPLIED. SNAP THE COVER ON THE CANISTER. MAKE PAPER-PUNCH SIZE HOLES IN THE TOP AND THE BOTTOM OF THE SECOND (OR MIDDLE) CANISTER. RUN THE STRING THROUGH THIS. PIERCE THE TOP OF THE THIRD CANISTER. THREAD THE STRING THROUGH THIS MAKING SURE THAT IT IS SECURE ENOUGH TO NOT PULL OUT WHEN UNDER PRESSURE. THE STRING, THROUGH THE MIDDLE CANISTER, SHOULD BE FREE TO MOVE EASILY. THE MIDDLE CANISTER ACTS AS A HANDLE WHICH THE SATELLITE SWINGER HOLDS OVERHEAD WHILE GENTLY SWINGING THE UPPER CANISTER. WEIGHTS (OF KNOWN QUANTITY) SHOULD BE ENCLOSED IN BOTH THE UPPER AND LOWER CAN-ISTERS. THE TOP CANISTER SHOULD BE SPUN IN A HORIZONTAL CIRCLE. DO THIS OUTDOORS. MAKE SURE THAT ALL STRING TIES ARE SECURE AND THAT NO ONE IS STANDING NEARBY WHEN YOU DO THIS. HOLD THE CAN-ISTER (CENTER ONE) IN ONE HAND, ABOVE YOUR HEAD. HOLD THE BOTTOM CANISTER WITH YOUR OTHER HAND. ROTATE THE TOP

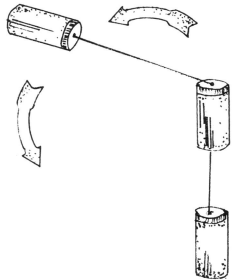

CANISTER IN SMALL CIRCLES SO AS TO SET THE THING IN MOTION. NOW SLOWLY LET GO OF THE CANISTER BEING HELD IN YOUR HAND. IF YOU

INCREASE THE SPEED OF ROTATION OF THE UPPER CANISTER, IT WILL
PULL THE BOTTOM CANISTER UP. SLOW IT DOWN AND SEE WHAT HAPPENS.
CHANGE THE WEIGHTS INSIDE THE CANISTER'S AND OBSERVE WHAT HAP-
PENS. TRY INCREASING THE BOTTOM CANISTER'S MASS. DECREASE THIS
AND INCREASE THE MASS OF THE TOP CANISTER. OBSERVE CHANGES.

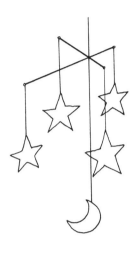

MYSTERY CONTAINERS

   USE AN OPAQUE CANISTER. PLACE ONE OBJECT INSIDE THE CON-
TAINER (START SIMPLE). CLOSE IT. HAVE CHILDREN, BY EXTERNAL MAN-
IPULATIONS OF THE CANISTER, DESCRIBE WHAT THEY INFER AS TO THE
CONTENTS OF THE CANISTER. SELECT OBJECTS THAT INHERENTLY POSSESS
ONE OR MORE UNIQUE PROPERTIES THAT WHEN PLACED IN THE CANISTER
COMMUNICATE SOME CLUE. A COTTON PUFF OR A RUBBERBAND WOULD BE A
POOR CHOICE. A STEEL BALL, BY CONTRAST, WOULD CONVEY MORE INFOR-
MATION. AS THE CHILDREN BECOME MORE PROFICIENT, ADD MORE OBJECTS
TO THE CANISTER.

THE 35mm MOTOR BOAT - AN OCEAN OF MOTION

YOU WILL NEED AN OPAQUE CANISTER, A SHORT LENGTH (ABOUT 3/4") OF (ABOUT 1/8") COPPER OR PLASTIC TUBING, A SELTZER TABLET, AND A SMALL CORK. ORIENTING THE CANISTER IN A HORIZONTAL POSITION, MAKE

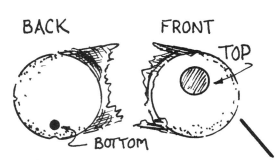

A HOLE IN THE LOWER PORTION OF THE BOTTOM TO ACCOMODATE THE SMALL DIAMETER TUBING. ALSO MAKE A HOLE IN THE TOP PORTION OF THE COVER. A 3/8" HOLE AND A SUITABLE SIZED CORK TO ACT AS A STOPPER WILL DO FINE. A CORK THAT WILL FIT TIGHTLY ENOUGH TO RESTRICT GAS FROM ESCAPING AND LOOSELY ENOUGH TO ACT AS A PRESSURE RELIEF VALVE SHOULD THE PRESSURE INSIDE THE CANISTER BECOME EXCESSIVE WOULD SERVE WELL. THIS CANISTER IS A PRESSURE CONTAINER AND IF THE EXHAUST BECOMES PLUGGED, GAS WILL BUILD UP AND IT WILL NEED TO BE RELEASED. THE POPPING CORK PROVIDES AN AUXILLARY OUTLET. SO, DO NOT JAM THE CORK IN THE 3/8" HOLE. SNUG IS GOOD! THE CANISTER NEEDS TO BE WEIGHTED DOWN SO THAT THE REAR END REMAINS SUBMERGED ALLOWING THE SHORT TUBING TO PERFORM AS A PROPULSION EXHAUST. THIS CAN BE ACCOMPLISHED BY INSERTING A SMALL COIN IN THE REAR BOTTOM OF THE CANISTER. THE CANISTER HAS A TENDENCY TO ROLL OVER IN THE WATER.

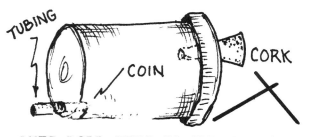

ADD, BY GLUING, ANTI-ROLL FINS TO THE SIDES. ADD SOME WATER. MAKE SURE THE CORK FITS SNUGLY INTO THE COVER. PLACE ONE QUARTER SELTZER TABLET INTO THE CANISTER. PLACE IT IN THE WATER. OBSERVE THE MOTION. WHAT CAN BE VARIED

TO EXPAND THIS INTO A VIABLE EXPERIMENT?

10

MEASURING THE AMOUNT OF WATER USED BY PLANTS

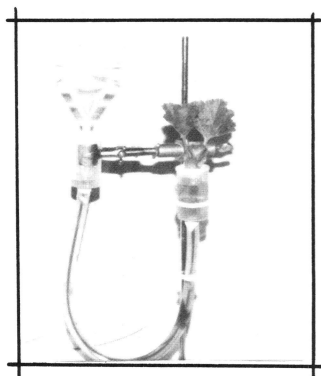

USE TWO, CLEAR 35mm FILM CAN-
ISTERS, SOME FLEXIBLE TUBING,
PLASTICENE CLAY, A FUNNEL AND A RING
STAND. CONNECT THE FUNNEL TO THE
SEALED GERANIUM CUTTING BY MEANS OF
THE TUBING. AT THE FUNNEL, ADD WATER
DAILY. MEASURE AND RECORD THE AMOUNT
OF WATER NECESSARY TO MAINTAIN THE
WATER LEVEL IN THE TUBE.

PULLEYS

GOOD SPOOL (PULLEY) OPERATION IS FACILITATED BY THE CONSTRUC-
TION OF GOOD SPOOL HOLDERS. USE GOOD WEIGHTS, WIRE CLOTHES HANGERS
CUT AND BENT AS NEEDED.

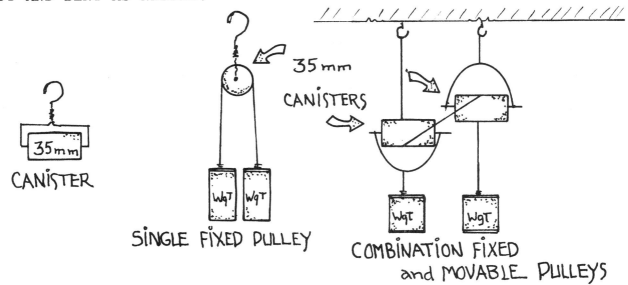

35 mm
CANISTERS

CANISTER

SINGLE FIXED PULLEY

COMBINATION FIXED
and MOVABLE PULLEYS

THE OBEDIENT CANISTER

PUNCH TWO HOLES IN TWO COVERS AND THE BOTTOM OF THE CANISTER. WITH ONE COVER PLACED AT EACH END OF THE CANISTER (PLACE THE FLAT SIDE OF THE COVER AGAINST THE BOTTOM) AND USING A PIPE CLEANER AS A RUBBERBAND THREADER, PASS A 3 - 4" RUBBERBAND THROUGH THE COVERS AND THE CANISTER BOTTOM FORMING AN INTERNAL "X" pattern. SLIP A RETAINER (MATCH STICK SEGMENT OR SOMETHING SIMILAR) IN PLACE SO THAT THE RUBBERBAND DOES NOT RE-TURN TO THE INTERIOR OF THE CAN-ISTER. KEEPING EVERYTHING IN-TACT, PULL THE COVER AWAY FROM THE CANISTER AND ATTACH A WEIGHT-ED OBJECT TO THE CENTER OF THE RUBBERBAND. CLOSE IT. ROLL IT. AS THE ENERGY FROM THE ROLL IS ACCUMULATED BY THE WINDING RUB-

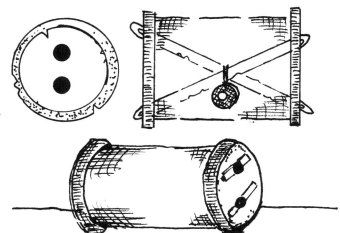

BERBAND AND THEN RELEASED, THE CANISTER WILL RETURN IN YOUR DIREC-TION. MEASURE BOTH DISTANCES. DOUBLE, TRIPLE THE MASS OF THE WEIGHTED OBJECT. INFER. ROLL THE OBEDIENT CANISTER. AGAIN, MEA-SURE BOTH DISTANCES. NOW, CHANGE THE RUBBERBAND. DOUBLE THE THICKNESS. DOUBLE THE NUMBER OF RUBBERBANDS. COMPARE THE RESULTS OF ONE, TWO, AND THREE RUBBERBANDS. CONSIDER OTHER VARIABLES. FORMULATE A PRIOR STATEMENT OF YOUR ANTICIPATED RESULTS. ROLL THE CANISTER. MEASURE. RECORD. GRAPH. SUPPORT OR REFUTE YOUR EARLIER STATEMENT. REMEMBER TO CONTROL ALL VARIABLES EXCEPT THE MANIPULATED VARIABLE.

RAMP ROLLERS

BECAUSE OF THE DIFFERENCES IN CIRCUMFERENCE OF EACH END OF THE SPOOL, A 35mm CANISTER DOES NOT ROLL IN A STRAIGHT LINE. THE COVERED END HAS A GREATER CIRCUMFERENCE. WHEN ROLLED FORWARD, THE CANISTER WILL BE PULLED TO THE SIDE WITH THE SMALLEST CIRCUMFERENCE. THE SMALLER CIRCUMFERENCE ACTS LIKE A FLAT TIRE ON A CAR AND PULLS TO THE DEFLATED TIRE SIDE. WHERE ON THE FRONT END OF A CAR SHOULD ONE PLACE HIS WORST TIRE (IT DEPENDS IN WHICH LANE YOU DO THE MAJOR PORTION OF YOUR DRIVING)? TO MAKE YOUR CANISTER ROLL IN A STRAIGHT LINE, GLUE A COVER TO THE SMALL END (FLAT SIDE OF COVER TO THE CANISTER). USING THREE CANISTERS, GLUE AN EXTRA COVER TO EACH ONE. SELECT AN INCLINED SURFACE. ROLL AN EMPTY CANISTER DOWN THE RAMP. OBSERVE. MEASURE THE DISTANCE IT ROLLED OUT BEYOND THE END OF THE RAMP. DETERMINE HOW FAST IT TRAVELED.

IN EVEN INCREMENTS, FOR EXAMPLE, 20g, 40g, OR 60g, ADD WEIGHTS TO EACH REMAINING CANISTER TO INCREASE THE MASS. MAKE A STATEMENT (HYPOTHESIS) THAT EXPRESSES YOUR EXPECTATIONS OF THE RESULTS EFFECTED BY THE CHANGES IN MASS. KEEPING THE ANGLE THE SAME AND ONLY VARYING THE MASS, ROLL EACH CANISTER DOWN THE RAMP. OBSERVE. RECORD. GRAPH YOUR RESULTS. INTERPRET THE GRAPH TO DETERMINE IF THE DATA SUPPORTS OR REFUTES YOUR PRIOR STATED HYPOTHESIS.

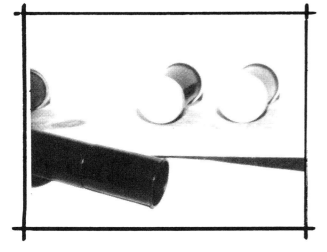

13

ADDITIONAL INVESTIGATIONS:

KEEP THE MASS CONSTANT, MANIPULATE (CHANGE) THE ANGLE OF THE RAMP.

KEEPING THE MASS AND THE ANGLE CONSTANT, MANIPULATE THE SURFACE TEXTURE OF THE RAMP, FOR EXAMPLE, WAXED SURFACE VS UNWAXED SURFACE, ETC.

DOUBLE 35mm CANISTER CAN BE CONSTRUCTED BY GLUING TWO CANISTERS TOGETHER.

SIPHONS

YOU WILL NEED TWO, CLEAR, 35mm CANISTERS, AND ABOUT 15 - 20" OF PLASTIC TUBING. CUT ONE HOLE IN EACH OF THE COVERS. THE DIAMETER OF THE HOLES SHOULD BE A BIT SMALLER THAN THE OUTSIDE DIAMETER OF THE TUBING ALLOWING FOR A SNUG FIT. INSERT THE TUBING. USE PLASTICENE CLAY OR SOME OTHER NON-NOXIOUS SEALANT TO EFFECTIVELY SEAL THE TUBING TO THE CANISTERS. A WATER TIGHT SEAL IS NECESSARY. ADD SUFFICIENT WATER TO THE SYSTEM TO ALLOW FOR MOVEMENT OF THE WATER AS THE CAN- 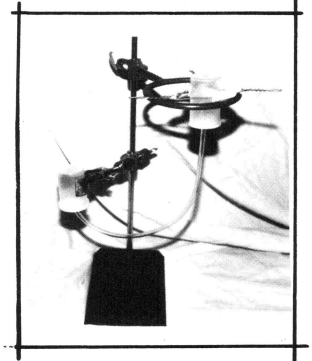 ISTERS ARE PLACED AT DIFFERENT LEVELS. CLOSE THE SYSTEM. YOUR SYSTEM SHOULD BE SELF CONTAINED AND READILY MOVEABLE FROM ONE LOCATION TO ANOTHER.

BUOYANCY

YOU WILL NEED THREE, CLEAR 35mm CANISTERS WITH SOME MARKINGS OR A SCALE TAPED ON THE VERTICAL SIDES OF EACH CYLINDER. ADD A KNOWN WEIGHT TO ONE OF THE CANISTERS. PLACE THE CANISTER IN TAP WATER. READ THE NUMERICAL VALUE OR NOTE THE MARKING ON THE VER- TICAL SCALE AS THE CANISTER FLOATS IN THE WATER. DOUBLE THE MASS OF THE SECOND CANISTER (ADD MORE BBs) AND PLACE THIS IN THE WATER. IN- FER WHAT THE SCALE READING WILL BE WHEN THIS CANISTER IS PLACED IN THE WATER. RECORD YOUR OBSERVA- TION. AGAIN, USING THE SAME

LIQUID TRIPLE THE MASS OF THE THIRD CANISTER. INFER WHAT THE SCALE READING WILL BE. RECORD YOUR OBSERVATION. COMPILE ALL THREE OB- SERVATIONS PLOTTING THEM ON A GRAPH. INTERPRET YOUR DATA. CAN YOU MAKE ANY CONCLUSIONS? PREDICTIONS?

WILL A 35mm CANISTER OF WATER FILLED TO THE BRIM SINK TO THE BOTTOM OF A CONTAINER FILLED WITH WATER? EXPLAIN YOUR OBSERVATIONS.

AN OBJECT WILL FLOAT, IRRESPECTIVE OF ITS DENSITY, IF IT IS LIGHTER THAN THE WEIGHT OF AN EQUAL VOLUME OF WATER THAT THE OBJECT DISPLACES. THE PLASTIC MATERIAL OF THE CANISTER IS LIGHTER THAN THE AMOUNT OF THE VOLUME OF WATER THAT THIS MATERIAL DISPLACES. HENCE, IT WILL FLOAT EVEN WHEN FILLED WITH WATER.

BUOYANCY CONTINUED

HOW BUOYANT IS A CLOSED 35mm CANISTER? PLACE A RUBBERBAND AROUND THE CANISTER. ATTACH A SMALL SWIVEL (FISHING) DEVICE TO THE RUBBERBAND. PLACE THIS IN WATER. IT WILL FLOAT. SUSPEND SUFFICIENT WEIGHTS TO THE SWIVEL DEVICE TO SINK THE CANISTER. OB- SERVE THE TOTAL WEIGHT NECESSARY TO SINK THE CANISTER. RECORD THIS WEIGHT. REPEAT THIS OPERA- TION USING TWO, 35mm CANISTERS

JOINED TOGETHER WITH A RUBBERBAND AND A SWIVEL ATTACHED TO IT. INFER THE WEIGHT NECESSARY TO SINK THIS. SINK IT BY ADDING SUF- FICIENT WEIGHTS TO THE SWIVEL DEVICE. RECORD THIS. REPEAT THIS USING THREE, 35mm CANISTERS JOINED TOGETHER. AGAIN, INFER THE WEIGHT NECESSARY TO SINK THESE THREE, JOINED CANISTERS. ADD THE NECESSARY WEIGHTS TO SINK THESE CANISTERS. OBSERVE, RECORD, AND GRAPH ALL THE DATA COLLECTED. HOW DID YOUR INFERENCES COMPARE TO THE RECORDED WEIGHTS NECESSARY TO SINK THE CANISTER IN EACH IN- STANCE? USING YOUR GRAPH, PREDICT WHAT WEIGHTS WOULD BE NECES- SARY TO SINK FOUR JOINED CANISTERS. VERIFY THIS. GENERATE A HY- POTHESIS FOR HOW THE BUOYANCY OF THESE VARIOUS CANISTERS WOULD BE EFFECTED BY THE PLACEMENT IN LIQUIDS OF DIFFERING DENSITIES, FOR EXAMPLE, THOSE LIQUIDS WITH A DENSITY OF LESS THAN 1 AND THOSE LIQUIDS WITH A DENSITY GREATER THAN 1.

SPOOLMOBILE - A MOVING EXPERIENCE

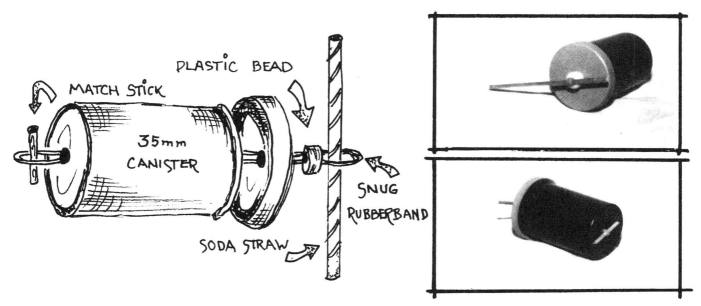

SPOOLMOBILES CAN BE CONSTRUCTED FROM ALMOST ANY HOLLOW CYLINDRICAL CONTAINER BE IT A COLA CAN, PILL BOTTLE, OATMEAL BOX, OR A TWO LITER PLASTIC BOTTLE. EACH SELECTION HAS ITS OWN UNIQUE ADVANTAGES AND DISADVANTAGES. HOWEVER, THE BASIC CONSTRUCTION IS THE SAME FOR ALL SPOOLMOBILES. CARE, UNIQUE TO EACH MATERIAL SELECTED, MUST BE OBSERVED IN THE PUNCHING, CUTTING, OR PIERCING OF HOLES OF CURVED PLASTIC SURFACES, METAL CAPS, INFLEXIBLE PLASTIC, ETC. EACH CONSIDERATION DICTATES A PRIME CONCERN FOR SAFETY.

WHEN COMPLETELY ASSEMBLED, CRANK UP THE SPOOLMOBILE. THIS PLACES ENERGY INTO THE SYSTEM. SOME OF THE VARIABLES ARE THE TYPE, SIZE, SHAPE, AND NUMBER OF RUBBERBANDS USED, THE SIZE, SHAPE, AND NUMBER OF THE BEADS USED, THE TYPE, LENGTH, AND SHAPE OF THE TRAILING RUDDER, THE SHAPE, SIZE, MASS, AND GENERAL CONFIGURATION OF THE SPOOL, THE SURFACE AND THE GRADIENT OF THE SURFACE, PLUS VARIATIONS IN THE NUMBER OF TURNS OF THE RUBBERBAND. ONE OR ALL OF THESE VARIABLES CAN BE INVESTIGATED. THINK. INFER. HYPOTHESIZE. OBSERVE THE ACTION. MEASURE THE RESULTS. RECORD (GRAPH) THE RESULTS. CONCLUDE AS TO THE SUPPORT OR THE REFUTATION OF YOUR PREVIOUSLY STATED HYPOTHESIS. VOILA!!

17

BUBBLE PIPE AND BLOW PIPE (BERNOULLI REVISITED)

YOU WILL NEED: A SODA STRAW, SOME CHEWING GUM (OR SOME OTHER NON-NOXIOUS SEALANT), AND A PING PONG BALL. USING A DEEP THROATED, ONE-HOLE PUNCH, MAKE A HOLE NEAR THE BOTTOM OF THE WALL OF THE CYL-INDER. INSERT THE STRAW, SEAL AROUND THE HOLE FOR AN AIR AND/OR LIQUID TIGHT SEAL. REMOVE THE TOP FROM THE CANISTER. FILL THE CONTAINER WITH BUBBLE-MAKING SOLUTION AT LEAST ABOVE THE INCOMING LEVEL OF THE STRAW. TOO MUCH SOLUTION WOULD BE MESSY. VOILA! A PERSONALIZED BUBBLE PIPE IS BORN. INCLINE THE STRAW SO THAT THE LIQUID DRAINS BACK DOWN INTO THE BOWL. CAUTION CHILDREN NOT TO SUCK IN THE LIQUID.

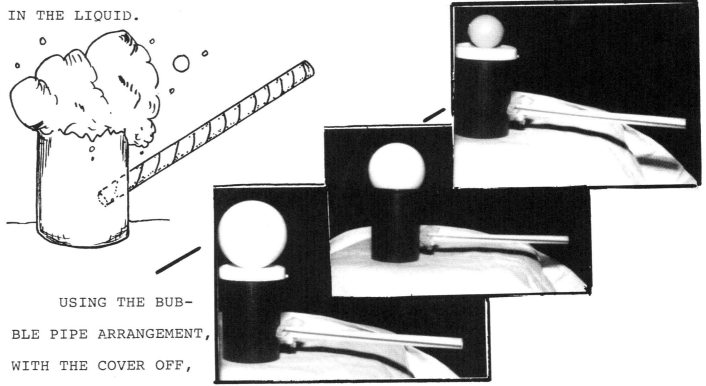

USING THE BUB-BLE PIPE ARRANGEMENT, WITH THE COVER OFF, PLACE A PING PONG BALL RECESSED INTO THE 35mm CANISTER. CAN YOU BLOW THIS BALL OUT OF THE CONTAINER? HOW HIGH CAN YOU BLOW THIS? CHECK WITH BERNOULLI. PLACE THE COVER, WITH A PAPER-PUNCH, SIZE HOLE LO-CATED IN ITS CENTER, ON THE CONTAINER. POSITION THE PING PONG BALL OVER THE HOLE. BALANCE IT GINGERLY WHILE BLOWING THROUGH THE PIPE (SEE THE ABOVE SKETCHES). OBSERVE. COMPARE YOUR OBSERVATIONS TO A SMALLER, LIGHTER-WEIGHT BALL.

18

MAKING 35mm FLASHLIGHTS

ONE CAN MAKE A ONE, TWO, OR MORE BATTERY FLASHLIGHT. TO CONSTRUCT A ONE BATTERY FLASHLIGHT, CUT TWO HOLES LARGE ENOUGH TO ACCOMODATE THE INSERTION OF ONE BRASS PAPER FASTENER, ONE TO EACH HOLE. THE HOLES SHOULD BE ONE ABOVE THE OTHER, MIDWAY UP THE VERTICAL WALL OF THE CANISTER. COPPER WIRE (BELL WIRE WORKS FINE) SHOULD BE JOINED TO THE BASE OF

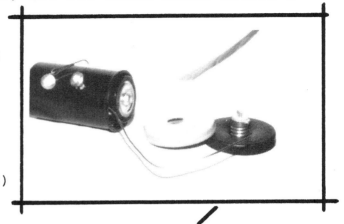

EACH OF THE FASTENERS. THIS SHOULD BE A VERY TIGHT WRAP. SOLDERING WOULD BE BETTER. IN ANY EVENT, THE COPPER WIRE WILL NEED TO BE STRIPPED OF ITS INSULATION WHERE THE WIRE JOINS THE BRASS FASTENER. SLIP A PAPER CLIP UNDER THE HEAD OF ONE OF THE FASTENERS. THIS SHOULD BE EXTERNAL TO THE CANISTER AND IT SHOULD SWIVEL SO THAT IT CAN ACT AS AN OFF OR ON SWITCH. PUSH THE WIRE AND THE BASE OF THE FASTENERS THROUGH THE HOLES. SPREAD THEM APART SO THEY CANNOT BE RETRACTED. THE WIRE ATTACHED TO THE LOWER FASTENER SHOULD BE SPIRALLY COILED TO ACT AS A SPRING CUSHION WHEN IN CONTACT WITH THE BASE OF THE "C" BATTERY WHEN IT IS INSERTED INTO THE CANISTER. THE WIRE FROM THE OTHER FASTENER SHOULD BE THREADED UP BETWEEN THE WALL OF THE CANISTER AND

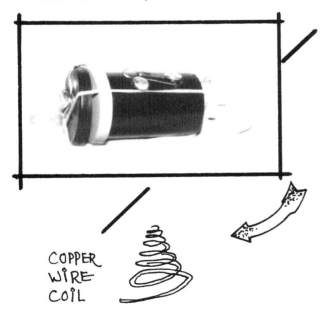

COPPER WIRE COIL

THE BATTERY. NOW WE ARE GETTING CLOSER TO COMPLETING THE CIRCUIT AND LIGHTING THE FLASHLIGHT. MAKE A PUNCH HOLE IN THE CENTER OF

TWO 35mm CANISTER COVERS. SNAP ONE COVER ON THE CANISTER AND
LOCK IT IN PLACE. THOSE 35mm CANISTERS WITH DOMED OR RAISED
COVERS WILL WORK BETTER THAN USING TWO, FLAT COVERS. HOWEVER,
SOMETIMES THEY ARE NOT ALWAYS AVAILABLE. SCREW THE BULB INTO AND

THROUGH THE HOLE IN THE SECOND
COVER. THE BASE OF THE BULB
SHOULD REST ON THE PROJECTED
PORTION OF THE TOP OF THE BAT-
TERY. USE RUBBERBANDS, TAPE,
ETC. TO TIE THIS ALL TOGETHER.
THE TOP WIRE SHOULD NOW BE MADE
TO TOUCH (TIGHTLY WRAP THE WIRE

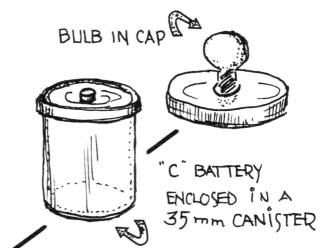

BULB IN CAP

"C" BATTERY
ENCLOSED IN A
35mm CANISTER

ABOUT THE SIDE OR THREADED PORTION) THE BULB. NOW USING YOUR PAPER
CLIP SWITCH, CLOSE THE CIRCUIT. THE LIGHT SHOULD GO ON - DIMLY.
USING THE SAME CIRCUIT CONSTRUCTION MAKE A TWO OR MORE BATTERY
FLASHLIGHT. A BRIGHTER LIGHT WILL BE OBSERVED.

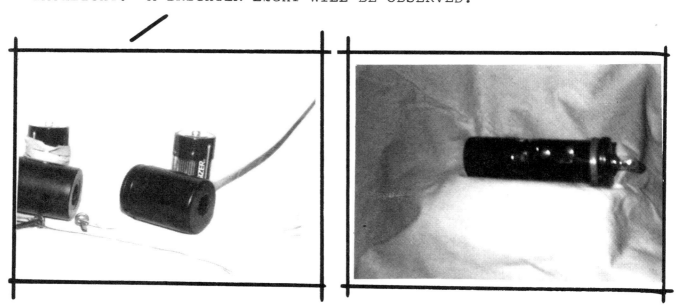

35mm CAMERA

YOU WILL NEED: WAX PAPER, ONE TOPLESS 35mm CANISTER, RUBBER-
BAND, AND A SMALL BIRTHDAY CANDLE PLUS ONE CANDLE HOLDER (ONE
PINCHED OR SCISSOR-TYPE CLOTHES PIN). PIERCE THE BOTTOM OF THE CAN-
ISTER MAKING A 2-3mm HOLE. CUT
A 10mm SQUARE OF WAX PAPER.
PLACE THIS OVER THE WIDE OPENING
AT THE TOP OF THE CANISTER. SNAP
A RUBBERBAND OVER THE WAX PAPER.

CANDLE HOLDER

THIS WILL BRING THE PAPER TIGHTLY OVER THE OPENING AND HUG THE CAN-
ISTER SMOOTHLY LIKE A DRUM COVER. CUT OR TRIM OFF THE EXCESS WAX
PAPER. USE THE PINCH TYPE, CLOTHES PIN TO HOLD THE CANDLE IN AN
UPRIGHT POSITION. LIGHT THE CANDLE. AT EYE LEVEL, HOLD THE AP-
PARATUS IN LINE AND BRING IT CLOSE TO THE FLAME. THIS TAKES SOME
MANIPULATION UNTIL THE CORRECT FOCUS IS ACHIEVED. VIEWING THROUGH
THE WAX PAPER YOU OBSERVE THE FLAME. THE CANDLE WILL NOT APPEAR
CLEARLY. THE KEY OBSERVATION IS TO NOTE THE DANCING FLAME AS IT IS

WAX PAPER

INVERTED FLAME

VIEWING END....

PROJECTED ONTO THE WAX PAPER
SCREEN. VIEWING THROUGH THE WAX
PAPER, YOU CAN OBSERVE THE FLAME
DANCING IN AN INVERTED IMAGE.
THIS CAN BEST BE OBSERVED IN A
DARKENED ROOM. LIGHT TRAVELS IN A STRAIGHT LINE. THIS INVERSION
CAN ONLY BE OBSERVED BECAUSE OF THIS PHENOMENON. RAYS OF LIGHT FROM
THE TOP PART OF THE CANDLE PASS THROUGH THE PINHOLE AND FALL ON THE
BOTTOM OF THE WAX PAPER. SIMILARLY, RAYS OF LIGHT FROM THE BOTTOM
PART OF THE CANDLE PASS THROUGH THE PINHOLE AND FALL ON THE TOP OF
THE WAXED PAPER. COMPARE OBSERVATIONS WHEN THE 35mm CAMERA IS
MOVED CLOSER AS OPPOSED TO FARTHER AWAY.

35mm GARDENS

OPAQUE CANISTERS MAKE EXCELLENT RECEPTACLES FOR GROWING SEEDS.

SMALL, SEED PLANTS SHOULD BE
UTILIZED, FOR EXAMPLE, RADISH,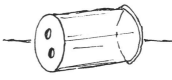
MARIGOLD, OR MUNG BEANS.
PUNCH SEVERAL DRAIN HOLES IN THE BOTTOM. ADD A
SMALL AMOUNT OF CRUSHED GRAVEL AND/OR CHARCOAL
TO THE BOTTOM OF THE CANISTER. ADD SOIL, PLANT
SEEDS, AND THEN WATER. VOILA!

CLEAR CANISTERS CAN BE USED TO INVESTIGATE ROOT GROWTH WHICH
CAN BE VIEWED EXTERNALLY.

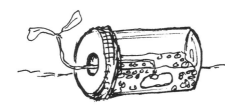

CLOSED OPAQUE CANISTERS, WITH A HOLE IN
THE COVER AND THE CONTAINER PLACED ON ITS SIDE,
CAN BE UTILIZED TO SHOW HOW PLANTS GROW
TOWARDS LIGHT.

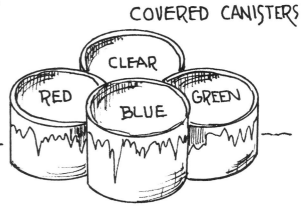

COVERED CANISTERS

GROUP TWO OR MORE CANISTERS TO-
GETHER. THESE CAN BE TAPED OR HELD
BY A RUBBERBAND. AFTER PLANTING THE
SEEDS, COVER THE TOP OPENING OF EACH
CANISTER WITH A DIFFERENT COLORED
CELLOPHANE, FOR EXAMPLE, RED, GREEN,
OR BLUE. MAINTAIN ONE CANISTER WITH A CLEAR CELLOPHANE COVERING
TO USE AS YOUR CONTROL. WITH ALL THINGS BEING MAINTAINED AS EQUAL
AND ONLY MANIPULATING THE COLOR OF LIGHT, DETERMINE WHAT EFFECT,
IF ANY, COLORED LIGHT HAS ON THE GROWTH OF PLANT SEEDS.

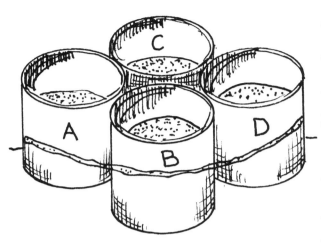

THIS SAME ARRANGEMENT OF CANIS-
TERS CAN BE UTILIZED WHEREIN EVERY-
THING IS HELD CONSTANT BUT THE TYPE
OF SOILS CAN BE VARIED. ADDITIONALLY,
AS ANOTHER INVESTIGATION, THE TYPE OF
LIQUID CAN BE VARIED, FOR EXAMPLE,
DISTILLED WATER, SALT WATER, TAP
WATER, POLLUTED WATER, ETC. CAN BE USED
AND COMPARED TO CONTROL SUCH AS RAIN
WATER.

FLOATABILITY / DENSITY

IN VARIOUS LIQUIDS, SOME THINGS FLOAT, SOME THINGS SINK, AND SOME THINGS REMAIN SUBMERGED SOMEWHERE BETWEEN THE SURFACE AND THE BOTTOM. WATER IS AN INTERESTING LIQUID. CONVENIENTLY IT HAS A DENSITY OF 1. DENSITY IS A RATIO BETWEEN MASS AND VOLUME. THIS RELATIONSHIP IS CONSTANT REGARDLESS OF THE AMOUNT AND SHAPE OF THE MATERIAL. DENSITY EQUALS THE MASS OF A MATERIAL DIVIDED BY ITS VOLUME. IN THE CASE OF WATER, ONE GRAM (MASS) OF WATER DIVIDED BY ITS VOLUME OF ONE mL EQUALS 1.

 $$DENSITY = \frac{MASS}{VOLUME} = \frac{1\ GRAM}{1mL} = 1.$$

ONE CUBIC CENTIMETER HAS A VOLUME THAT COULD BE OCCUPIED BY 1mL OF WATER.

THE FACT THAT WATER HAS A DENSITY OF 1 MAKES THIS NUMERICAL VALUE VERY USEFUL IN THE STUDY OF SCIENCE. THE DENSITY OF WATER (1) IS A REFERENCE POINT FOR THE COMPARISON OF OTHER MATERIALS. MATERIALS THAT FLOAT IN WATER POSSESS A DENSITY OF LESS THAN 1. MATERIALS THAT SINK IN WATER HAVE A DENSITY GREATER THAN 1. MATE- RIALS THAT ARE PARTIALLY SUBMERGED HAVE A DENSITY THAT IS VERY CLOSE TO BUT EXCEEDS THAT OF WATER. A CUBIC CENTIMETER (cc) OF WHITE PINE WOOD HAS A DENSITY OF ABOUT 0.6. IT FLOATS. FROZEN WATER (ICE) FLOATS IN WATER. WHAT CAN YOU INFER ABOUT ITS DENSITY? A CUBIC CENTIMETER OF COPPER WITH A DENSITY OF 8.92 WILL NOT FLOAT. COPPER IS SAID TO BE 8.92 TIMES HEAVIER THAN WATER PER UNIT VOLUME.

SEA WATER (SALT WATER) BECAUSE OF THE PRESENCE OF DISSOLVED SOLIDS IS SLIGHTLY DENSER THAN PURE, FRESH WATER. SEA WATER HAS A DENSITY OF ABOUT 1.026 - 1.028. OIL HAS A DENSITY OF LESS THAN 1 (ABOUT 0.9), HENCE IT FLOATS ON WATER.

24

THE HYDROMETER

YOU WILL NEED ONE COMPLETE, CLEAR 35mm CANISTER, A SMALL PLASTIC SCALE (OR A PAPER ONE ENCASED IN PLASTIC TAPE FOR WATER-PROOFING PURPOSES), BBs OR PLUMBER'S CHAIN TO BE USED FOR WEIGHTS.

TAPE THE SCALE VERTICALLY ON THE SIDE OF THE CANISTER. ADD THE WEIGHTS TO THE CANISTER. CAP THE CANISTER. PLACE YOUR HYDRO-

METER IN WATER. IT SHOULD FLOAT UPRIGHT, IF NOT, YOU MAY NEED TO ADD MORE WEIGHTS. OBSERVE WHERE THE WATER LEVEL MARK STRIKES YOUR VERTICAL SCALE. RECORD THIS. REMOVE THE CONTAINER. DRY IT. USING SOME INSOL-UBLE MARKER, MAKE A MARK AT THE PREVIOUSLY OBSERVED WATER-LEVEL MARK. THIS BE-COMES YOUR "ZERO" MARK ON YOUR SCALE. THE HYDROMETER

CAN NOW BE PLACED IN VARIOUS LIQUIDS. THE "ZERO" MARK COULD APPEAR ABOVE THE LIQUID, BELOW THE LIQUID, OR AT THE SAME POINT AS WHEN FLOATING IN WATER. SALT WATER IS MORE DENSE THAN TAP WATER. WILL THE HYDROMETER FLOAT LOWER IN THE SALT WATER? WHAT DOES INCREASED SALINITY DO TO THE LEVEL OF FLOATATION OF THE HYDROMETER? TRY DIF-FERENT LIQUIDS. CONSTRUCT A DENSITY SCALE OF VARIOUS LIQUIDS. WHAT EFFECT DOES CHANGING THE TEMPERATURE OF THE LIQUID HAVE ON THE LEVEL OF FLOATATION?

SOUND, COLOR MIXTURES, AND SUBJECTIVE COLOR

YOU WILL NEED STRING, TWO 35mm CANISTER TOPS, GLUE, PLASTICENE CLAY, AND TWO WOODEN DOWELS. GLUE THE TWO TOPS TOGETHER (FLAT SIDE TO FLAT SIDE). PUNCH TWO HOLES THROUGH THE GLUED, TWO TOPS. THE TOPS WILL RESEMBLE A TWO-HOLED BUTTON. RUN THE STRING THROUGH THE HOLES AND ATTACH THEM TO THE DOWELS (DRILLED HOLES IN THE DOWELS WILL HELP). TWO TOPS ARE SUGGESTED BECAUSE ONE TOP WILL NOT PROVIDE SUFFICIENT MASS TO ACCOMPLISH THE DESIRED TASK. IT IS

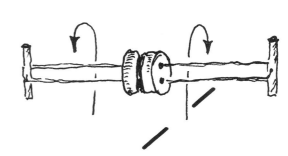

FURTHER SUGGESTED THAT PLASTICENE CLAY BE FIRMLY PRESSED INTO THE EXPOSED RECESSES OF THE TOPS TO PROVIDE ADDITIONAL MASS. MAKE SURE THE CLAY DOES NOT CLOG THE HOLES.

SPIN THE COVERS IN A VERTICAL PLANE ALLOWING THE STRING TO BECOME WOUND UP. PULL BACK ON THE DOWEL HANDLES ALTERNATELY REWINDING AND UNWINDING THE STRING. KEEP THE TOPS SPINNING BY ESTABLISHING A SIMPLE RHYTHM. A SOUND WILL BE PRODUCED. WHAT ARE THE VARIABLES? HOW CAN THESE BE FURTHER INVESTIGATED?

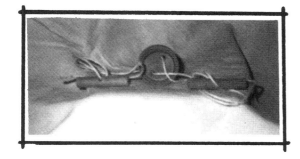

USING THE BACK-TO-BACK TOPS, GLUE TO EACH SIDE A CIRCULAR DISC CUT FROM A MANILA FOLDER. THE DISC SHOULD HAVE RADIAL SEGMENTS ALTERNATELY PAINTED RED AND GREEN. SPIN THIS DEVICE RAPIDLY. THE MIXTURE OF THESE TWO COLORS, REFLECTED TO THE EYE BY THE SPINNING DISC, WILL APPEAR AS YELLOW.

INSTEAD OF USING COLOR TO REPRODUCE COLOR, WE CAN REPRODUCE COLOR BY USING WHITE AND BLACK. CUT A WHITE DISC TO FIT ONTO EACH

SIDE OF THE TWO-HOLE TOPS. INK IN (BLACK INK) ONE HALF OF EACH

DISC. ATTACH AND SPIN THESE DISCS RAPIDLY. WHAT COLORS DO YOU

OBSERVE? YOU SHOULD OBSERVE CONCENTRIC CIRCLES TINTED WITH DIF-

FERENT COLORS. WHAT ADDITIONAL VARIABLES CAN BE INVESTIGATED?

REVERSE THE DIRECTION OF SPIN. CHANGE THE BLACK AND WHITE PAT-

TERNS. WHAT EFFECT DOES THE SPEED OF ROTATION HAVE ON THE COLORS

VIEWED? VIEW THIS UNDER MOONLIGHT, DIFFUSED LIGHT, ARTIFICIAL

LIGHT SUCH AS FLOURESCENT OR ORDINARY LIGHT BULBS.

SPECTROSCOPE

TO SHOW A SPECTRUM, YOU WILL NEED A COMPLETE 35mm CANISTER AND SOME TRANSMISSION DIFFRACTION GRATING (13,400 GROOVES PER INCH). FROM THE TOP COVER OF THE CANISTER, CUT OUT A 10-15mm DIAMETER CIRCLE. INSIDE THE COVER GLUE A PIECE OF DIFFRACTION GRATING SUFFICIENT TO COVER THE 10-15mm OPENING. AT THE CENTER OF BOTTOM OF THE CYLINDER, PUNCH A SMALL 3-4mm OPENING. CLOSE THE CYLINDER. LOOK UP AT A FLOURESCENT LIGHT THROUGH THE DIFFRACTION GRATING END OF THE CYLINDER. THE SMALL 3-4mm OPENING WILL BE POINTING UP AT THE LIGHT. ROTATE THE CYLINDER UNTIL YOU NOTICE A SPECTRUM CAUSED BY THE INCOMING LIGHT SEPARATED BY THE DIFFRACTION GRATING. WHAT, IF ANY, RESULTS DO YOU THINK MOONLIGHT WILL CAUSE?

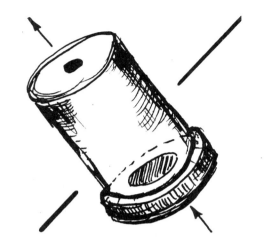

AWAY IN THE DRAY - A 35mm EXPERIENCE

YOU WILL NEED TWO, EIGHT INCH LENGTHS OF 1/4" WOOD DOWELING, ONE 35mm CANISTER, SEVERAL WOODEN STICKS, AND TWO RUBBERBANDS.

TAPER ONE END OF THE WOODEN DOWELS SO THAT THEY MAKE A SMOOTH, ANGULAR JOINT WHEN JOINED. GLUE THESE TOGETHER. ABOUT 1/4" FROM THE OPPOSING ENDS, MAKE A SMALL NOTCH ON THE OUTWARD SIDE OF THE DOWELS. THESE WILL ACT AS RECESSES FOR THE RUBBERBANDS. GLUE SEVERAL, WOOD CROSSMEMBERS TO MAKE THE SYSTEM RIGID. WHEN THIS IS DRY AND RIGID

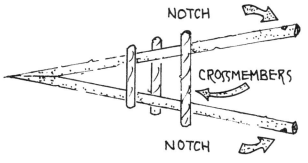

ATTACH THE 35mm CANISTER TO THE DOWELS. THE CANISTER SHOULD HAVE A HOLE PUNCHED IN THE COVER AND THE BOTTOM OF THE CANISTER PLUS ONE HOLE IN THE ADDED COVER WHICH IS GLUED (FLAT SIDE TO THE BOTTOM). NEXT, THREAD TWO RUBBERBANDS (ONE FROM EACH DOWEL THROUGH THE COVERS) INTO THE CANISTER. INSERT A PORTION OF A MATCHSTICK TO RETAIN THE RUBBERBAND INSIDE THE CANISTER. A SMALL DROP OF GLUE APPLIED TO THAT POINT WHERE THE RUBBERBANDS NEST AGAINST THE DOWELS WILL ANCHOR THE DRAY MOTOR (CANISTER).

YOU MAY NEED TO INSERT A WEIGHT INSIDE THE CANISTER TO INCREASE THE MASS OF THE MOTOR. WIND UP THE CANISTER. CLOCKWISE VS COUNTER CLOCKWISE GIVES DIFFERENT RESULTS.

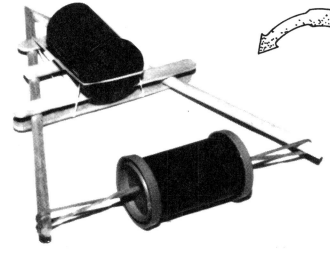

YOUR 35mm DRAY CAN BE MADE TO PULL VARIOUS WEIGHTS PLACED ON THE CROSSMEMBERS. HOW MUCH WEIGHT PER GIVEN NUMBER OF CANISTER TURNS WILL THE DRAY PULL? WHAT CAN BE DONE TO REDUCE FRICTION AND INCREASE THE PULLING POWER? WHAT EFFECT DOES INCREASING THE MASS OF THE CANISTER HAVE?

35mm STRING TELEPHONE

YOU WILL NEED TWO, 35mm CANISTERS AND A TWENTY-FIVE-FOOT LENGTH OF HEAVY THREAD. PIERCE THE CENTER OF THE BOTTOM OF EACH CANISTER. INSERT THE ENDS OF THE THREAD THROUGH THE BOTTOM POR-TION OF THE CANISTERS. KNOT THE THREAD AROUND A SMALL, PORTION OF A TOOTHPICK OR MATCHSTICK TO PREVENT THE THREAD FROM PULLING OUT.

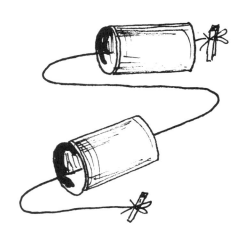

TWO CHILDREN ARE NECESSARY TO OPERATE THE 35mm TELEPHONE. ONE PER-SON TRANSMITS AND ONE PERSON RECEIVES THE MESSAGE. THEN THE ROLES ARE RE-VERSED. THE THREAD MUST BE DRAWN TAUT AND IT MUST NOT BE ALLOWED TO TOUCH ANY OBJECT. HAVING MET THESE CONDITIONS, HAVE ONE CHILD SPEAK INTO THE TRANSMITTING CANISTER AND THE OTHER CHILD PLACE HIS EAR AGAINST THE RECEIVING CANISTER PLUS COVERING THE OTHER EAR WITH ONE'S HAND TO SHUT OUT EXTERIOR NOISES. VIBRATIONS FROM THE CHILD SPEAKING INTO THE TRANSMITTER WILL CAUSE A VIBRATION IN THE BOTTOM

(DIAPHRAGM) OF THE CANISTER (THE TRANSMITTER). THE CHILD ON THE RECEIVING END SHOULD HEAR THE MESSAGE.

VARIABLES THAT COULD BE IN-VESTIGATED ARE: LENGTH OF THE THREAD; TYPE OF THREAD; THE USE OF THREAD VS STRING OR OTHER MATERIALS; SIZE OF THE TRANSMITTER; SHAPE OF THE TRANSMITTER; THE CONSTRUCTION OF A PARTY LINE SYSTEM. CAN A THIRD PARTY BE ADDED TO THE TELEPHONE SYSTEM?

BUOYANCY - the 35mm canister floatometer

BUOYANCY IN LIQUIDS OF VARYING DENSITIES CAN BE MEASURED AND COMPARED TO EACH OTHER USING THE 35mm FLOATOMETER. TRACE THE CIRCUMFERENCE OF THE BASE OF A 35mm CANISTER ON A PLASTIC COVER (OLEO TUB OR A PEANUT CAN COVER). CAREFULLY CUT OUT THE ENCLOSED CIRCLE. INSERT A TOPLESS CANISTER IN THE OPENING. FLOAT THE FLOATOMETER IN A CONTAINER OF TAP WATER. WHILE IN THE FLOATING POSITION,

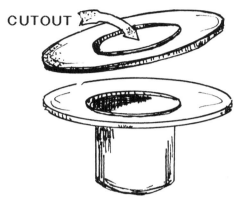

CUTOUT

PLACE METAL WASHERS, ONE AT A TIME, INTO THE 35mm CANISTER. EACH, ONE-INCH, METAL WASHER WEIGHS APPROXIMATELY SEVEN GRAMS. WHEN 4-5 WASHERS ARE ADDED TO THE INTERIOR OF AN EMPTY, 35mm CANISTER (DEVOID OF THE PLASTIC COLLAR), IT WILL SINK IN TAP WATER. AN

EMPTY 35mm CANISTER, INSERTED INTO THE PLASTIC COLLAR, WILL SINK IN TAP WATER WHEN APPROXIMATELY 12 METAL WASHERS ARE ADDED TO THE INTERIOR OF THE CANISTER. HOW MIGHT ONE ACCOUNT FOR THIS DIFFERENCE?

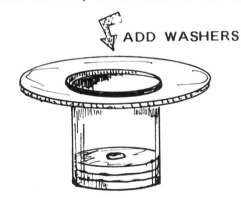

ADD WASHERS

USE THIS SAME NUMBER (12) OF WASHERS AS YOUR BASE OR FRAME OF REFERENCE. ASSIGN A VALUE OF 1 TO TAP WATER. ALL FUTURE MEASURES WILL BE COMPARED TO THIS. EITHER THINGS ARE LESS DENSE THAN 1 AND FLOAT IN TAP WATER, MORE DENSE THAN 1 AND SINK IN TAP WATER, OR THEY ARE EQUAL IN DENSITY AND BARELY SUBMERGE THEMSELVES IN TAP WATER BUT DO NOT SINK TO THE BOTTOM OF THE CONTAINER.

IF YOU USE A FLOATOMETER IN A LIQUID THAT REQUIRED 24 WASHERS TO SINK THE CANISTER APPARATUS, THEN YOU COULD ASSIGN THIS LIQUID A VALUE OF TWO, INASMUCH AS IT TAKES TWICE AS MANY WASHERS TO SINK THE FLOATOMETER. WE WOULD SAY THAT THIS LIQUID IS TWICE AS DENSE AS TAP WATER. IF IT TOOK 36 WASHERS TO SINK THE FLOATOMETER, WE WOULD SAY THAT THIS LIQUID IS THREE TIMES AS DENSE AS TAP WATER AND IS IDENTIFIED AS HAVING A NUMERICAL VALUE OF 3. CALCULATIONS CAN BE MADE FOR

THE NUMBER OF WASHERS THAT FALL INBETWEEN EVEN INCREMENTS SUCH AS 12, 24, AND 36, FOR EXAMPLE, 18 WASHERS WOULD HAVE A COMPARATIVE VALUE OF 1 and 1/2 (18 DIVIDED BY 12). THE DENSITY OF THIS LIQUID BEING MEASURED AND COMPARED WOULD BE SAID TO BE 1 and 1/2 TIMES AS DENSE AS TAP WATER. WHAT WOULD BE THE DENSITY OF A LIQUID IN WHICH IT TOOK ONLY 6 WASHERS TO SINK THE FLOATOMETER?

USING A PLASTIC TUB COVER, CUT TWO HOLES TO RECEIVE TWO, TOPLESS 35mm CANISTERS. FLOAT THIS APPARATUS IN TAP WATER. INFER HOW MANY WASHERS IT WOULD TAKE TO SINK THE TWO-CANISTER, 35mm FLOATOMETER APPARATUS. SINK THE AP-

PARATUS. RECORD THE NUMBER OF WASHERS IT TOOK TO ACCOMPLISH THIS TASK. COMPARE THIS NUMBER TO THE NUMBER OF WASHERS NECESSARY TO SINK A SINGLE-CANISTER, 35mm FLOATOMETER AP-PARATUS. IS THERE A DIFFERENCE? REPEAT THIS COMPARISON, COMPARING A THREE-CANISTER, 35mm FLOATOMETER APPARATUS. DOES IT TAKE THE SAME NUMBER OF WASHERS TO SINK EACH AP-

PARATUS? MAKE A GRAPH RECORDING THE RESULTS OF THE NUMBER OF WASHERS NECES-SARY TO SINK A ONE, TWO, AND THREE-CANISTER 35mm CANISTER FLOATATION APPARATUS. WHAT KIND OF A CURVE DOES THE PLOT OF YOUR DATA LOOK LIKE?

USING ANY VARIETY OF THE 35mm CANISTER, FLOATOMETER APPARATUSES (ONE, TWO, OR THREE CANISTERS), COLLECT MEASURES OF BUOYANCY IN OIL, MOLASSES, RAIN WATER, SALT WATER, AND/OR DISTILLED WATER. RANK ORDER THESE LIQUIDS IN ORDER OF LEAST BUOYANT TO MOST BUOYANT.

DOES THE TEMPERATURE OF LIQUIDS EFFECT THE BUOYANCY OF PARTICULAR LIQUIDS?

INSECT CONTAINER

USE A <u>CLEAR</u> OR <u>NEARLY</u> CLEAR CANISTER. DISCARD THE CANISTER COVER.
DRILL SEVERAL, SMALL (1/16th or 1/32nd of an inch) AIR HOLES IN THE CANISTER.
BE CAREFUL WHEN DOING THIS! DRILLING ON A CURVED SURFACE CAN BE DANGEROUS
INASMUCH AS A SPINNING DRILL BIT HAS A TENDENCY TO DANCE OFF THE CURVED SURFACE
OF THE CANISTER DURING THE DRILLING PROCESS. TO AVOID THIS, USE A NAIL AND
SCRATCH A SMALL "X" AT THOSE POINTS YOU WISH TO DRILL. THIS ENABLES THE DRILL
BIT TO GET A START ENABLING IT TO STAY IN THE DESIRED POSITION DURING THE DRIL-
LING PROCESS. A LARGE DOWEL OR THE END OF A BROOM HANDLE PLACED INSIDE THE
CANISTER PRIOR TO DRILLING STABILIZES THE CANISTER AND MAKES DRILLING THE HOLES
A SMOOTHER AND SAFER OPERATION. <u>NEVER</u> HOLD THE CANISTER IN YOUR HAND WHILE
DRILLING OR ATTEMPTING TO PIERCE THE CANISTER WITH A SHARP OBJECT. ANY TOOL
SLIPPAGE COULD CAUSE INJURY TO YOU OR SOMEONE ELSE. IF AVAILABLE, USE A BENCH
VISE TO HOLD THE 35mm CANISTER DURING ANY DRILLING ACTION. WITH CARE, AND OB-
SERVING ALL THE PRECAUTIONARY MEASURES, THIS ACTION IS A SIMPLE PROCEDURE.

insect container

USING A 1 and 1/4 INCH METAL PUNCH,
CUT OUT FOAM-RUBBER CYLINDERS THAT ARE
APPROXIMATELY 1 and 1/2" (OR ABOUT 3cm)
HIGH. THESE CYLINDERS WILL FIT SNUGLY INTO
THE 35mm CANISTER. USING A 1/4 INCH METAL
PUNCH, PUSH IT HALF WAY THROUGH THE CENTER
OF THE UPRIGHT, FOAM-RUBBER CYLINDER. WITH
SOME MANUVERING OF THE METAL PUNCH CUT OUT
THE 1/4 INCH PLUG ALLOWING IT TO SEPARATE
OUT HALF WAY THROUGH THE LARGE CYLINDER.

THIS LEAVES A VOID FOR A STRAW, DOWEL, OR A STUBBY PENCIL. GLUE THIS HANDLE
IN THE CYLINDER HOLE. VOILA! YOU NOW HAVE A SLIDING, BUG-TIGHT CYLINDER THAT
CAN HOUSE INSECTS FOR CLOSE OBSERVATIONS. IF YOU DO NOT HAVE A 1/4 INCH METAL
PUNCH, CAREFULLY INSERT A POINTED PENCIL INTO THE FOAM-RUBBER CYLINDER AND GLUE
IT.

FOAM-RUBBER CYLINDERS

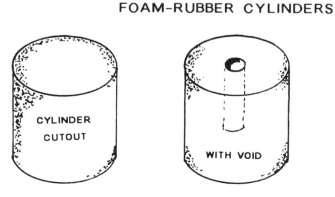
CYLINDER CUTOUT

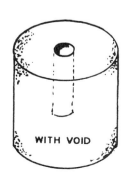
WITH VOID

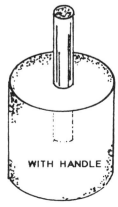
WITH HANDLE

CIRCULAR MOTION - on a roll

A CLOSED, 35mm CANISTER WILL NOT ROLL IN A STRAIGHT LINE. BECAUSE OF DIFFERENCES IN THE DIAMETERS OF THE CIRCULAR, TERMINAL ENDS OF THE CANISTER, WHEN THE CANISTER IS PLACED IN MOTION, IT WILL VEER OFF IN ONE DIRECTION. AND, IF SUFFICIENT ENERGY IS PLACED INTO THE SYSTEM, IT WILL TRACE A CIRCLE AS IT ROLLS ON A FLAT SURFACE. THE 35mm CANISTER WILL VEER OFF IN THE DIRECTION OF THE LARGER, DIAMETER END OF THE CANISTER.

INFER THE DIAMETER OF A CIRCLE THAT WILL BE FORMED BY THE PATH SET BY YOU AS YOU PLACE THE 35mm CANISTER IN MOTION.

CHANGE THE DIAMETER OF ONE END OF THE 35mm CANISTER BY GLUING A LARGER CIRCULAR-SHAPED OBJECT TO ONE OF THE ENDS.

HOW DOES THE PATH OF THE 35mm CANISTER WITH THE LARGER DIAMETER DISC GLUED TO ONE END COMPARE TO THE PATH OF THE REGULAR 35mm CANISTER WHEN BOTH ARE ROLLED IN THE SAME PATH IN THE SAME MANNER?

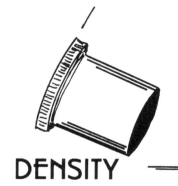

IF THE COMPARED DIFFERENCES BETWEEN CANISTERS WITH VARYING, TERMINAL-END DIAMETERS WERE OBSERVED AND RECORDED USING CONSISTENT GRADUATIONS (for example, 2" diameter, 3" diameter, and 4" diameter), WHAT WOULD A GRAPH OF THE RESULTANT CANISTER-CIRCLE TRACES (diameters) LOOK LIKE? WHAT VARIABLES MIGHT INFLUENCE THE RESULTS OF SUCH A COMPARISON?

DENSITY ——————— COLUMN

IF A LIQUID DOES NOT MIX WITH WATER, IT IS POSSIBLE TO FIND OUT IF IT IS MORE OR LESS DENSE THAN WATER.

USE A <u>CLEAR</u> OR <u>NEARLY CLEAR</u> 35mm CANISTER THAT ALLOWS YOU TO SEE WHAT IS GOING ON INTERNALLY. FILL THE CONTAINER, A BIT SHY OF THE TOP, WITH 1/3 WATER, 1/3 MOLASSES, AND 1/3 COOKING OIL. CAP THE CONTAINER AND SHAKE IT GENTLY. OBSERVE THE RATE OF LIQUID SEPARATION. WHAT IS THE ORDER OF THE LIQUIDS (BOTTOM TO TOP)? WHICH LIQUID HAS THE GREATEST DENSITY? THE LEAST DENSITY?

ADD TO THE CONTAINER A SMALL PEBBLE, A PIECE OF CARDBOARD, AND A PIECE OF PARAF-FIN FROM A CANDLE. CAP THE CONTAINER AND SHAKE IT GENTLY. IN WHAT POSITION WITHIN THE CONTAINER DO THESE THREE OBJECTS END UP? HOW DO THE DENSITIES OF THESE OBJECTS COMPARE TO THE DENSITIES OF THE THREE LIQUIDS?

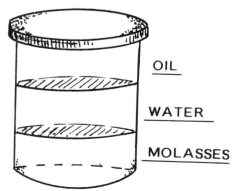

OIL

WATER

MOLASSES

RECIPROCAL, PENDULUM MOTION

FILL TWO, 35mm CANISTERS WITH EQUAL AMOUNTS OF SAND, CLAY, OR WASHERS. WEIGH THESE CONTAINERS TO DETERMINE THAT THEY ARE OF EQUAL MASS.

MAKE A HOLE IN THE CAP OF EACH CANISTER. THREAD A STRING THROUGH THE HOLE IN EACH CONTAINER COVER. KNOT THE STRING SO THAT THE STRING CANNOT PULL OUT OF THE CONTAINER COVER.

HANG EACH CANISTER FROM A CROSSBAR. SEPARATE THE TWO, PENDANT CANISTERS FROM EACH OTHER BY POSITIONING A NOTCHED DOWEL (OR SODA STRAW) BETWEEN THEM.

WITH THE APPARATUS AT REST, SET CANISTER "A" IN MOTION. OBSERVE WHAT HAPPENS TO CANISTER "A" AND THEN TO CANISTER "B".

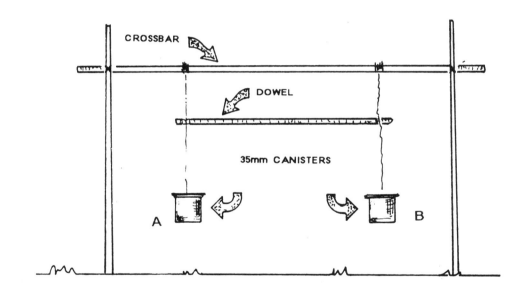

OSCILLATIONS BY CANISTER "A" ARE TRANSFERRED THROUGH THE NOTCHED DOWEL (OR SODA STRAW) TO CANISTER "B" AND CANISTER "B" IS SET IN MOTION. THIS PROCESS OF RECIPROCAL TRANSFER OF ENERGY FROM "A" TO "B" AND THEN BACK FROM "B" TO "A" WILL CONTINUE UNTIL ALL THE ENERGY IN THE SYSTEM IS SPENT.

THE INCLINED RIDER

MAKE A SMALL HOLE (about 1/16th of an inch) IN THE CENTER OF A 35mm CANISTER COVER. USING A PAPER CLIP, STRAIGHTEN OUT ONE END AND PUSH THIS THROUGH THE HOLE IN THE CANISTER COVER. HAVING DONE THIS, BEND THE WIRE SO THAT IT CANNOT BE READILY PULLED OUT OF THE HOLE. SNAP THE COVER ON THE CANISTER.

35mm canister rider

STRETCH A PIECE OF STRING OR FISHING LINE BETWEEN TWO ANCHOR POINTS OF DIFFERING ELEVATIONS. MAKE SURE THAT THE LINE DOES NOT INTERFERE WITH THE CLASSROOM TRAFFIC PATTERN OF CHILDREN IN YOUR CLASSROOM. INASMUCH AS CHILDREN AND ADULTS DO NOT EXPECT LINES TO BE STRUNG THROUGHOUT THE CLASSROOM, THEY SHOULD AND MUST BE FOREWARNED OF THIS CON-DITION. PRACTICE SAFE SCIENCE AND LOCATE YOUR STRING LINE OR LINES AWAY FROM CROWDED AREAS, WARN INDIVIDUALS OF THE PRESENCE OF THESE LINES, AND DO NOT LEAVE THE ROOM WITH THESE LINES IN PLACE WITHOUT HANGING REMOVABLE STREAMERS FROM THE LINES ENABLING INDIVIDUALS TO BE AWARE OF THEM.

OPEN THE CANISTER AND ADD WEIGHTS. DETERMINE THE MASS OF THE COMPLETE 35mm CANISTER APPARATUS. USING THE PAPER CLIP AS A HANGING DEVICE, ATTACH THE CANISTER TO THE TAUT, STRING RUNWAY. AT THE HIGH END OF THE STRING RUNWAY, RELEASE THE CAN-ISTER. RECORD HOW LONG A PERIOD OF TIME IT TAKES THE CANISTER TO TRAVEL THE FULL MEASURED DISTANCE OF THE STRING (or some

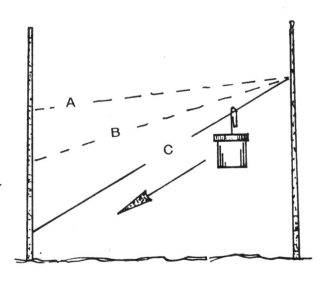

pre-established, measured distance, for example, 1 meter). CALCULATE THE VELOCITY OF THE CANISTER'S DESCENT. VELOCITY IS THE DISTANCE TRAVELED DIVIDED BY THE TIME IT TOOK TO TRAVEL THAT DISTANCE.

ADDITIONAL ACTIONS:

QUESTIONS		ACTIONS

• DOES INCREASED MASS EFFECT VELOCITY? VARY THE MASS OF THE CANISTER KEEP THE ANGLE CONSTANT

• DOES INCREASING THE ANGLE OF DESCENT EFFECT THE VELOCITY OF THE MOVING CANISTER? VARY THE ANGLE OF THE INCLINED STRING KEEP THE MASS OF THE CANISTER CONSTANT

DOES REDUCING THE FRICTION OF THE LINE OR STRING EFFECT THE TIME OF DESCENT? TRY VARIOUS RUNWAY MATERIALS, FOR EXAMPLE, YARN, ROUGH STRING, SYNTHETIC STRING, ETC.

RECORD YOUR OBSERVATIONS. COLLECT PERTINENT DATA. PLOT YOUR COLLECTED DATA ON A GRAPH. INTERPRET THE DATA IN LIGHT OF YOUR QUESTION OR HYPOTHESIS. DOES YOUR EVIDENCE SUPPORT OR REFUTE YOUR QUESTION OR HYPOTHESIS?

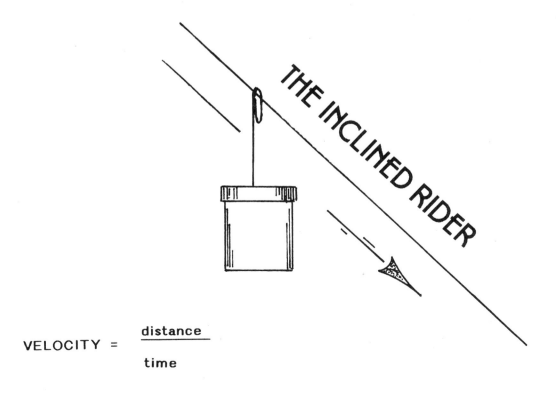

THE INCLINED RIDER

$$\text{VELOCITY} = \frac{\text{distance}}{\text{time}}$$

CONSTRUCTING A 35MM KALEIDOSCOPE

KALEIDOSCOPES COME IN A WIDE VARIETY OF SHAPES, SIZES, AND COMPLEXITIES. THE 35mm CANISTER KALEIDOSCOPE IS OF SIMPLE CONSTRUCTION. TO CONSTRUCT YOUR 35mm CANISTER KALEIDOSCOPE YOU WILL NEED TWO, COMPLETE 35mm CANISTERS - ONE CLEAR AND ONE OPAQUE. THE CLEAR CANISTER WILL SERVE AS A RECEPTACLE FOR THE OBJECTS THAT WILL BE ROTATED AND VIEWED. CUT (or punch*) A ONE-INCH HOLE IN THE COVER OF THE CLEAR CANISTER. THIS DIMENSION IS NOT CRITICAL. WHAT THIS CUTOUT DOES IS TO RID THE COVER OF THE CLEAR CANISTER OF ITS IRREGULARITIES.

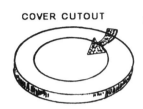
COVER CUTOUT

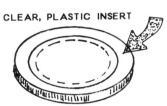
CLEAR, PLASTIC INSERT

THIS CUTOUT AREA NEEDS TO BE COVERED WITH A CLEAR DISC. THUS, A DISC, SLIGHTLY LARGER THAN THE ONE-INCH HOLE, NEEDS TO BE CUT FROM A PIECE OF THIN, CLEAR PLASTIC. GLUE THIS DISC INSIDE THE COVER. INASMUCH AS THERE ARE MANY DIFFERENT KINDS OF GLUE AND MANY DIF-FERENT KINDS OF PLASTIC CANISTER MATERIALS, ASK YOUR HOBBY SHOP PERSON FOR A RECOMMENDATION FOR JOINING PLASTIC TO PLASTIC. ADD TO YOUR CONTAINER PLASTIC SHARDS (AVAILABLE AT MOST HOBBY AND CRAFT SHOPS), SEEDS, BEADS, BUTTONS, BITS OF COLORED STONES, ETC. IT WILL TAKE SOME MANIPULATION OF THE FINISHED AP-PARATUS TO PERMIT YOU TO JUDGE JUST "HOW MUCH" IS SUFFICIENT FOR YOUR KALEI-DOSCOPE. MATERIALS CAN BE READILY INCREASED, DECREASED, ALTERED, OR SUB-STITUTED. CLOSE THE CONTAINER. YOU ARE FINISHED WITH THE TOP HALF OF YOUR KALEIDOSCOPE.

CUT, PUNCH, OR SNIP OUT A 3/4ths OF AN INCH HOLE IN THE COVER OF THE OPAQUE CANISTER. CUT OUT A TRIANGLE FROM THE BASE OF THE 35mm CANISTER. THIS IS ACCOMPLISHED BY MAKING A SMALL HOLE AND THEN ENLARGING THIS TO THE DE-

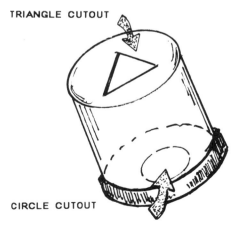
TRIANGLE CUTOUT

CIRCLE CUTOUT

SIRED TRIANGLE SHAPE BY SLOWLY AND CAREFULLY SNIPPING UNWANTED MATERIAL AWAY. THE TRIANG-ULAR CUTOUT SIZE SHOULD MATCH, BUT NOT EX-CEED, THE SIZE OF THE (LATER TO BE INSERTED) TRIANGULAR CANISTER INSERT. THE TRIANGULAR INSERT MUST BE CONSTRUCTED OF A REFLECTIVE MATERIAL AND SHOULD BE SHAPED INTO AN EQUI-LATERAL, TRIANGULAR PRISM. EACH ANGLE SHOULD MEASURE SIXTY DEGREES. EACH OF THE THREE, REFLECTIVE COMPONENTS THAT MAKE UP THE CANISTER INSERT SHOULD MEASURE 7/8ths OF AN INCH BY 1 and 1/2 INCHES BY 3/32nds OF AN INCH THICK. THESE PIECES ARE POSITIONED TO FORM A TRIANGULAR PRISM.

* ARCH PUNCHES CAN BE PURCHASED FROM MACHINE TOOL SUPPLY COMPANIES OR JEWELRY SUPPLY HOUSES.

THESE PIECES SHOULD BE WRAPPED WITH TAPE OR MASKING TAPE TO ASSIST IN THE RETEN-
TION OF THIS PRISM SHAPE. THESE THREE
PIECES CAN BE MADE FROM MIRROR GLASS,
SHINY REFLECTIVE METAL, OR THIN, STIFF
CARDBOARD INDIVIDUALLY WRAPPED IN HEAVY-
DUTY ALUMINUM FOIL (SHINY SIDE EXPOSED).
THE DIMENSIONS AND THE ANGLES ARE THE SAME
REGARDLESS OF THE MATERIALS YOU ELECT TO

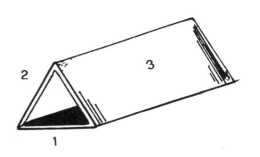

USE.   THE USE OF MIRRORED GLASS WOULD PROVIDE THE BEST RESULTS.   HOWEVER, MIRROR
GLASS MUST BE CUT BY A PROFESSIONAL GLASS CUTTER.   ONCE GLASS IS INCORPORATED IN-
TO THE SYSTEM, SPECIAL CARE MUST BE OBSERVED TO INSURE THE SAFETY OF CHILDREN.
SHINY ALUMINUM SHEET WORKS WELL.   IT CUTS EASILY, BUT ALL EDGES MUST BE DEBURRED
AND SMOOTHED OVER BEFORE USING IT.   THE ALUMINUM, FOIL-COVERED, CARDBOARD IS THE
SIMPLEST CANISTER INSERT TO MAKE AND THE SAFEST FOR YOUNG CHILDREN TO MANIPULATE.
WHEN FORMING THE TRIANGULAR INSERT, LAY OUT THE PIECES ON A FLAT SURFACE AND
JOIN THEM TOGETHER WITH TAPE ON THE MIRROR-LESS SIDE LEAVING SPACE BETWEEN EACH
PIECE TO ALLOW FOR THE HINGING MOTION THAT IS
NEEDED TO FORM THE TRIANGULAR PRISM.

        PLACE THE TRIANGULAR INSERT INSIDE
THE CANISTER.   INVERT THE CONTAINER.
PUSH THE INSERT SNUGLY UP TO THE TRIANGULAR
CUTOUT.   THE TRIANGULAR-COVER CUT SHOULD
PARALLEL THE TRIANGLE SIDES OF THE INSERT.

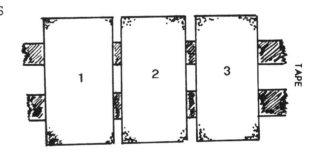

AS A SAFETY MEASURE, COVER EACH END OF THE OPAQUE CONTAINER WITH A CLEAR, PLASTIC
DISC.   GLUE THESE IN PLACE.   SNAP THE BOTTOM COVER ON.   IN THIS ORIENTATION, IN-
VERT AND PLACE THE CLEAR CANISTER ON TOP OF THE TRIANGULAR CUTOUT PORTION OF THE
OPAQUE CANISTER.   YOU SHOULD BE VIEWING THROUGH THE CLEAR DISC OF THE UPPER CAN-
ISTER HOLD THE COMPLETE APPARATUS UP TO THE
LIGHT AND KEEPING THE BOTTOM CANISTER STATION-
ARY, ROTATE THE TOP HALF OF THE APPARATUS.

        ROTATION AND TILTING OF THE APPARATUS
WILL ALLOW THE CONTENTS OF THE TOP CANISTER
TO SPILL AROUND AND BE REFLECTED IN THE IN-
DIVIDUAL REFLECTIVE SURFACES OF THE CANISTER'S
INSERT.   A PANORAMA OF CHANGING, COLORED PAT-
TERNS SHOULD BE VISIBLE.

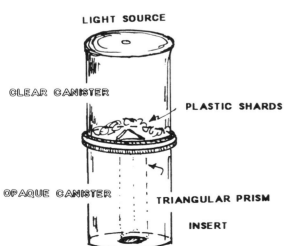

LIGHT SOURCE

CLEAR CANISTER

PLASTIC SHARDS

OPAQUE CANISTER

TRIANGULAR PRISM

INSERT

INDEX